UNDER THE CURSE

Goethe's *Iphigenie amongst Taurians*

In a new version by

Dan Farrelly

Carysfort Press

A Carysfort Press Book

Under the Curse

A new version of Goethe's *Iphigenie auf Tauris* by Dan Farrelly

First published in Ireland in 2000 as a paperback original by Carysfort Press, 58 Woodfield, Scholarstown Road
Dublin 16, Ireland

Reprinted 2007
© 2007 Dan Farrelly
Dan Farrelly has asserted his right to be identified as the author of this work

Typeset by Carysfort Press
Cover design by Brian O'Connor
Printed and bound by eprint limited
35 Coolmine Industrial Estate, Blanchardstown, Dublin 15
Ireland

This book is published with the financial assistance of
The Arts Council (An Chomhairle Ealaíon), Dublin, Ireland

ISBN 978-1-904505-30-3

Note: the German text I have followed is that of the Hamburger Ausgabe, vol. 5.

I acknowledge with pleasure my indebtedness to my family, friends, colleagues, and students, whose warmth, integrity, friendship, and loyalty over the years have mirrored all that I find good in Goethe's Iphigenie.

D.F.

Introduction:

The modernity of Goethe's *Iphigenie*

Euripides, born about 2,230 years before Goethe, was considered relatively modern in his own era, when he completed *Iphigeneia in Tauris*, c.414 BC. In his relationship to the gods he is obviously pre-Christian, and Goethe, by the time he completes his *Iphigenie* in 1786, is no longer Christian but post-Christian. But in what sense is Goethe post-Christian and what is the relevance to the play of this 'post-Christianity'?

For Goethe, the relationship between Iphigenie and the gods is defined by recourse to the biblical notion that we are made in the image of God. Iphigenie, who sees herself as set aside by the gods to lift the curse of killing within her family, cannot simply prevent the killing of her brother Orestes by a trick she is asked to play on Thoas, the King. She is not capable of lying to the man who has befriended her and who, in fact, loves her. The central question of Goethe's play is that of personal integrity. To lie to Thoas – even to save her life – would amount to a perversion of herself, and, because she is made in the image of the gods, it would amount to a perversion of *their* image. Hence, when faced with the dilemma of either lying to Thoas or risking execution of Orestes, Pylades, and herself, she calls on the gods to save her and to save their own image within her. Caught up in this dilemma, she fears that the hatred her ancestors bore the Olympian gods will rise up in her, blinding her as it blinded her ancestors, and continuing the mad cycle of hatred and killing – which constitutes the curse on her family.

For Euripides, both the problem and the solution are quite different. Here Iphigenie herself, when given the chance to save her brother and to escape from Tauris, thinks up a plan to deceive the Taurians. It is full of lies about the statue of the goddess turning around on its pedestal because of the presence of a matricide in the temple. The plan fails when the escape ship is washed back onto shore and all are captured. The safety of the Greeks is secured through the intervention of Athena herself, who persuades Thoas that he must free them. Like the gods themselves, Thoas must bow to necessity.

For Goethe's Iphigenie, fate and necessity are not dominant. When Goethe's Thoas invokes necessity as binding through his country's laws, Iphigenie claims his necessity is of purely human invention. Men must learn that the gods themselves are not bent on destruction. (Cf. the various modern forms of 'religious' war!) She claims the right to hear the voice of the gods speaking within her, even when it contradicts the man-made laws to which Thoas is appealing. We recognize here the independent stance of the Martin Luther tradition; but Goethe has also moved much further on to a post-Christian, personal ethic, which does not look to Christ as the Redeemer from sin but which calls on the individual to act with human integrity.

In this context, the relationship between Thoas and Iphigenie undergoes profound development in Goethe's play. In Euripides' play, Thoas does not actually appear till roughly the last quarter of the play and, when he mentions Iphigenie, his words sound merely impersonal and official: 'Where is the Hellene woman who guards this temple? Has she already performed the first rites over the strangers? Are their bodies already brightly burning within the holy shrine?' These words he speaks to the chorus. Then follows the confrontation with Iphigenie herself, in which she lies to him about the statue.

Goethe's version could hardly be more different. Early in the first act of Goethe's five-act play, Arkas, Thoas' minister, is preparing Iphigenie for a visit from Thoas and hinting that

Thoas is becoming more insistent in his attentions to her. Not
realizing that it is marriage he has in mind, Iphigenie passionately
gives vent to her outraged feelings. When, in scene three, Thoas
makes his honourable intentions clear and asks her to be his
bride and queen, the first element of her dilemma is revealed.
His desire to keep her at Tauris conflicts with her desire to
return home to help in the lifting of her family's curse. The fact
that she does not reciprocate his love complicates the issue.
That she reveres him as a father and sees him as her friend does
not help. His feelings are hurt and he is resentful. At this point,
the second element of the dilemma emerges, where he
announces, vengefully, that two strangers have been captured
and that now she should fulfil the duties of her office and make
arrangements for their sacrifice – according to the ancient laws
which, under her influence, he has too long held in abeyance. As
a punishment for her refusal to marry Thoas, she is now, in fact,
being required to execute her brother and hence continue the
curse of killing under which her family has lived for generations.
Of course, at this particular point, she is not yet aware that one
of the strangers to be executed is her brother, Orestes.

Euripides offers, understandably, a less humanistic picture of
Iphigenie. She is, in fact, involved in the sacrificing of strangers
though not directly in their execution. Goethe's Iphigenie
manages to convince Thoas to ignore the barbaric custom
altogether. Next, in Euripides' play, after Iphigenie dreams that
Orestes is dead, her heart is hardened and she longs for revenge:
she wishes that Helen of Troy or Menelaus – both of whom she
holds responsible for her plight – would be captured and
delivered over to her: 'Then might I have revenge and pay them
back.' Goethe's Iphigenie has no such thoughts of revenge.
Again, Euripides' Iphigenie is the inventor of the plot and the
web of lies to deceive Thoas. In Goethe's version, she has the
plot forced on her by Pylades and ultimately refuses to co-
operate. Instead, she puts her trust in Thoas' love for her and in

his humanity. Finally, in Goethe a different view of woman's dignity shines through. When Euripides has Iphigenie state that she is prepared to die to save her brother and thus ensure the continuance of his line, part of her reasoning is: 'There is no doubt about it: a man's death is a sore loss to a house, a woman's is of little account.' Her acceptance of this view is unthinkable for Goethe's Iphigenie, though she does focus, with regret, on the inferior social role allotted to women.

The role of Athena, the *deus ex machina*, at the end of Euripides' play needs mentioning here. The problem for Iphigenie and Orestes is solved by the intervention of Athena saying that it is the wish of her brother, Apollo, that the statue be returned to Greece and that Orestes be allowed to return home. Iphigenie is given instructions about how the rest of her life is to be spent: in service to the goddess in the sacred terraces of Brauron where she will die and be buried. Thoas, too, is given his instructions: he is to let them go and not be angry. By contrast, in Goethe's play the decree of the gods plays no direct role. The gods speak to people not by external decree but in human hearts. Iphigenie appeals to the gods to justify her in her truthfulness and in her trust in the innate goodness of another fellow human being — even though he be the barbarian king, Thoas.

Because for Goethe the gods are no longer exterior but have withdrawn into the human heart, the problems of all the characters do not stem directly from the gods' actions — whatever about the origins of the curse. The problem of the play and its solution concern the two central characters: Iphigenie and Thoas. As drama, this must be highlighted.

The fact that Goethe, in writing *Iphigenie auf Tauris*, was displaying his interest in a classical type of theatre, has, I think, misled traditional interpreters into associating the Iphigenie figure with a Greek statue, as if what you see on the surface is beautiful and harmonious but that Iphigenie is lacking in vitality. Such interpretations probably do scant justice to Greek statues, and, to my mind, they also fail to understand the depth and darkness of the tensions on which Goethe's play is built. It would seem that, in choosing a mythological subject, Goethe removed himself from the concrete social and political challenges of his generation. After all, the play was completed in the years immediately preceding the French Revolution, and the abuses people suffered under feudal society were as real in the Weimar Duchy as they were elsewhere in Europe. A further problem seems to be that there is very little external action in the play – perhaps an indication that the play is mainly psychological.

With regard to the mythological subject: it is possible to kill the play for a modern audience by retaining all the details from the long story of the myth – from the beginning with Tantalus right down to the arrival of Orestes at Tauris. But these can be pared down to the essentials, using just enough detail to show that the curse on Iphigenie's family continues to work from generation to generation. In my version of the play I have not only stripped it down in this way but also given it the title 'Under the Curse'. I think that is a strong enough statement to make the play resonate with similar situations – in Ireland and in Europe, and even further afield, where a new generation inherits problems from previous generations and either continues to live them out or struggles to solve them. To make the play relevant to a modern world you don't have to resort to extremes in dress and stage set.

The lack of so-called external action is not necessarily a major problem. Apart from the fact that, in Act Five, Orestes arrives on the scene with his sword drawn, the physical skirmishes happen off-stage: the capture of Orestes and Pylades near the beginning of the play and the final capture of the ship reported in Act Five. It is clear that, if the play is to live, it must live largely off the dialogue, and that the dialogue has to be based on psychological tensions which are recognisable as part of our modern life. The production of Goethe's play has to guarantee that the plot gathers momentum and that the tension mounts to an almost unbearable degree for Iphigenie when she sings the song of the fates at the end of Act Four. Faced with the dilemma of betraying Thoas or destroying the Greeks, tempted to despair of the gods – to curse them and accept that her family is cursed – Iphigenie is at breaking point. This is no cold, marble statue, Greek or otherwise. Of course, the significance of her solution can be debated. With regard to her truthfulness, her openness to Thoas, her humanity – we could ask: are these acceptable solutions to the conflict? But at least Goethe doesn't look *outside* the world of our experience for a solution. Nor does he see that lies and cunning have a role to play – the tactics employed in Euripides' play and suggested by Pylades in Goethe's play. The solution depends on people and on the way they decide to relate to one another. Much hinges on the integrity of a small group of people, on their ability to build trust. Integrity and trust are the solution offered by Goethe in his play two hundred years ago. In this sense, the play poses a problem for society at the beginning of the new millennium.

Under the Curse was first produced by the Gate Theatre in London in 2003. It was directed by Joe Hill-Gibbins.

The cast was as follows:

Iphigenie   Catherine McCormack

Thoas   Peter Guinness

Arkas   Michael Thomas

Orestes   Aidan McArdle

Pylades   Tom Smith

Peter Guinness as Thoas and Catherine McCormack as
Iphigenie in the Gate (London) performance of *Under the Curse*.
Photo: Pau Ros. Courtesy of the Gate Theatre.

Characters

Iphigenie, daughter of Agamemnon and Clytemnestra

Thoas, King of the Taurians

Arkas, minister of King Thoas

Orestes, brother of Iphigenie

Pylades, friend of Orestes

All the scenes take place in a grove in front of Diana's temple at Tauris.

Synopsis: Iphigenie, believed to have been sacrificed by her father, Agamemnon, has been saved by the goddess, Diana, and brought to the barbarian land of Tauris, where she is installed as priestess in Diana's temple.

Though protected, honoured, and loved by King Thoas, she rejects his offer of marriage because she hopes to return home to heal the curse on her family: Agamemnon's act in sacrificing his daughter is, in fact, the continuation of a curse which has dogged his family for generations.

At the outset of the play, Iphigenie does not know that the curse has gone even further. In revenge for Iphigenie's sacrifice, Clytemnestra, her mother, has killed Agamemnon on his return from the Trojan War. In revenge for the murder of his father, Orestes has killed his mother. Orestes, himself needing to be liberated from the avenging furies, has been sent by Apollo to the temple in Tauris. He and his friend Pylades are captured by King Thoas' men and delivered over to the priestess, Iphigenie, to be sacrificed to Diana.

The curse of murder within Agamemnon's family seems about to be continued – sister is now required to murder brother. Iphigenie is now 'under the curse'.

ACT ONE

Scene One

Iphigenie alone.

Iphigenie: I enter the rich-leafed shadow cast by the living
Peaks around this holy place, Diana's temple,
And thrill to its feel, forever new, though never
Able to see it as my home.
I yield these many years, obey the higher force
That keeps me here obscure, estranged,
Oceans apart from my beloved.
I pass the days here standing by the shore,
In heart and mind beyond the sea, united with my own,
And in reply the swish and thump of heavy waves
Invades my ears.

Whatever smile might form upon my lips
Is shaded by this deeply rooted sorrow;
My thoughts go down, down to the region
That was home, where the sun first opened
Up for me the skies,
Where, born together, we played and gently formed the ties,
The bond that since could ride within the heaving swell
Of time's great ocean-like expanse.

It's not for me to wrangle with the gods.
Yet noble Thoas holds me here.
There's no escape from duty's grasp.
I feel with shame, Diana, my heart resist your will.
You gave me safety in this distant land
Yet here I chafe where I should serve you still.

Scene Two

Enter Arkas enthusiastically.

Arkas: I come from the King. He bids me bring his greetings
To the priestess of Diana, for on this day
Tauris must thank the goddess anew
For shining victories in battle.
The King, triumphant with his army,
Will soon appear.

Iphigenie: *with reserve.* He will be worthily received.
The goddess will accept with grace
Whatever Thoas brings in sacrifice.

Arkas: But what about the honoured priestess of Diana?
If only in her gaze we saw a brighter,
Gleaming light of welcome. Take back
The veil, that sad reserve that year by year
Obscures from us your heart.
Some steely band – I see it in your eyes –
Defends from us the inner secrets of your soul.

Iphigenie: A fate well known to refugees and exiles.

Arkas: And that is how you see yourself in Tauris?

Iphigenie: What foreign country can be home to us?

Arkas: By now you'd be a stranger in your own land.

Iphigenie: The very reason why I bleed.
I was a child and hardly had begun
To know my father, mother, brother, sisters
When I was torn from them by an iron hand.

Why speak of the joy that grows with early youth?
Though rescued, no zest for life could
Penetrate the cloud that has descended on me.

Arkas: If you see yourself as wretched as you say,
What of the thanks you owe to Thoas?

Iphigenie: Thoas will always have my thanks.

Arkas: But not the gratitude he has deserved.
Where is the look of joy, the sign of your contentment,
Your affection?
It's many years since you were destined for this temple
Where Thoas found you sent us by the gods.
He showed respect, affection. The custom of
Sacrificing strangers on these altar steps
Was not applied to you.

Iphigenie: To draw the breath of life is not enough.
Why should I dedicate my life to casting shadows
Around this my grave? You think that's joy
And self-fulfilment? Preparing every day
For those grey years where, turned away from life
You forget all else except the memories of the dead?
A fruitless life amounts to early death.

Arkas: Such noble pride! What you achieve
Does not content you. This I understand.
And yet, I pity you: your zest for life is gone.
But see, since your arrival here, what you have done.
Who has brought the King such joy?
Whose gentle voice has stayed the violent
Hand that puts all strangers to the sword
In bloody sacrifice?
Who often saved our prisoners from certain death

And sent them homeward bound?
Does not Diana, yielding to your prayers,
Forego her prize?
Victory now attends our wars,
And Thoas, no longer just a leader,
Has grown milder through your presence.
Your life is fruitless? Your gentle hand
Has changed the fate of thousands.
In you Diana gave this people a sparkling
Fount of joy. For strangers here, instead of death
You've been protection, the hope of a safe return to home.

Iphigenie: Such little feats escape the gaze
Of those who see what's left to do.

Arkas: Could you find words of praise
For those who spurn what they achieve?

Iphigenie: It's worse to dwell upon your deeds.

Arkas: It's just as bad, with pride,
To underrate one's value as vainly to promote
An empty cause.
You see me as an honest man?
You know my loyalty to you?
Then listen carefully to what I say:
When speaking with the king today,
Smooth the path of his approach.

Iphigenie: Your well-intended kindness
Frightens me. I often have to be evasive
With the king.

Arkas: Reflect on what you do, what's good for you.
Since Thoas lost his son he trusts but few

And of these few there's none he really trusts.
He sees in every son of noble birth a threat,
A claimant to his throne. He fears old age
Will see him lonely, helpless.
He fears the prospect of revolt, a violent death.
In Tauris words don't count for much,
For Thoas least of all. He knows how
To command, to act. Achieving hidden aims
By tortuous, diplomatic speech –
This art he doesn't know.
Don't make it hard for him,
Don't hide behind reserve.
Be open, show him you understand.

Iphigenie: And lay myself open to a threat?

Arkas: In his attentions you can see a threat?

Iphigenie: The worst I can imagine.

Arkas: Reward his affection with your trust.

Iphigenie: When I no longer need to be afraid.

Arkas: Why do you conceal from him your origin?

Iphigenie: What priestess doesn't have her secrets?

Arkas: But secrets from the king?
Though he is undemanding, he feels it deep within
That you conceal yourself from him.

Iphigenie: He harbours resentment? He is annoyed with me?

Arkas: I imagine so. Not that he says it.
Sometimes he lets slip a word that tells me
To possess you is his dearest wish.
Don't leave him to himself,
Don't let grim thoughts gain ground
In him. You could regret it, you could
Look back too late to my advice.

Iphigenie: What!? Thoas thinks to do
What no noble man, with any self-respect
Or reverence for the gods would countenance?
He plans to drag me from the altar to his bed?
I call on all the gods, and on the resolute Diana
Who will protect her priestess, and as a virgin,
Protect another virgin from this rape!

Arkas: Calm down! The king's blood is not so wild.
His grim determination, which I sense,
Is aimed at something else.
I beg you, confide in him,
Show him gratitude at least,
If that's as far as you can go.

Iphigenie: Please, tell me: there's something else you know.

Arkas: He'll tell you himself. I see him coming.
You honour him, and your own heart
Tells you to bring him your friendship and trust.
His noble mind will open to your gentle word. *Exit*

Iphigenie: I don't see how to follow such advice.
But for his generosity I can reward the mighty king –
If I find words which serve the truth
And still find favour with the man.

Scene Three

Enter Thoas.

Iphigenie: May Diana bless you, Thoas, with every gift
She thinks befits a king – amongst them
Victory, fame, and riches,
Prosperity for your people,
Fulfilment of your every pious wish.
As caring ruler set above the many,
May happiness be your lot beyond all measure.

Thoas: Happiness? (*Pointedly*) Good-will shown the ruler
Would bring some satisfaction.
What I've achieved means more to others
Than to me. The highest happiness,
For king or subject, is centred on his home.
You shared my sorrow
When savage war destroyed my dearest son.
Revenge, as long as it preoccupied my mind,
Distracted from the void within myself.
But now, returning home, my son avenged,
My enemies destroyed, their lands laid waste,
What greets me here? What joy is left?
In every eye I read no more the acceptance
Of my reign, but worry and unease
About the future.
They see a king without a son and heir.
They bow to me because they know they must.
In visiting this temple now I cherish but one wish,
To you not strange or unexpected:
My people will exult, I will rejoice,
If you agree to be my bride.

Iphigenie: Your offer, Thoas, is too much

For one you know so little.
It shames this fugitive whose only wish
Already you've fulfilled: I wanted peace,
A haven, and these you have bestowed on me.

Thoas: The secret of your origin you should
At last explain. No king, no country should
Accept such reticence from you.
The dictates of necessity, our laws
Strike terror in each stranger's heart.
But you we have received with open arms,
No privilege has been withheld,
You spend your time as freely as you wish.
Your host expects, deserves from you
Some openness in return.

Iphigenie: If I've concealed from you, O King,
My origin, my family's name,
This was not mistrust but sense of shame.
To tell you of the curse upon my head,
To show you who it is you nourish and protect
Might fill with horror such a noble heart.
Instead of offering me a place beside you
On your throne, you might drive me out –
To wretchedness. Instead of awaiting here
The joyful hour that ends the years of exile,
I would be banished.
What can a refugee expect? -
Exposure to cold hearts and savage hands.

Thoas: The gods can think of you
This way or that, may plan for you and yours
A dire fate. But since the day of your arrival here
And you have lived in safety in our midst,
I know that blessings from above

Have here abounded.
How can I think my priestess
Is laden down with guilt?

Iphigenie: These blessings are your own reward, not mine.

Thoas: No blessing comes to those who help the guilty.
Give up your reticence and speak.
Don't say I make unjust demands.
It was a goddess who delivered
You up to me. Sacred you were to her,
Sacred to me. Let her decide your fate:
If there is hope of your returning home,
Then *my demands* are void.
But should *your hope* be void
And if your race is scattered
Or by some disaster is wiped out,
Then you are mine on many counts.
Speak openly. You know I'll keep my word.

Iphigenie: A long held silence is hard for me to break.
A secret shared has left its safe abode
To harm or heal, depending on the gods.
My secret? My family descends from Tantalus!

Thoas: Tantalus! How can you be so calm and tell me that?
The man you claim as ancestor was formerly
A favourite of the gods. You mean the Tantalus
Who sat with Jupiter in council and at table?
The man whose words of wisdom, like oracles,
Delighted even gods?

Iphigenie: Yes, that's the one. But why do gods
Pretend that men can be their equal?
The human race is much too weak –

It has no head for dizzy heights.
This man was not ignoble, certainly no traitor.
While not born to be a servant,
He was too frail to live with thunderbolts.
His mistake was human, and he was sternly judged.
According to the poets, his downfall came
From arrogance and treachery.
Cast out by Jupiter, in shame
He was a denizen of hell.
Now his descendants share in his disgrace.

Thoas: *His* disgrace – is Tantalus the only one to blame?

Iphigenie: His sons and grandsons inherited his titanic
Might and heart. As for their minds:
The gods locked out the light.
Who could then be prudent, moderate, wise and patient?
Their blindness led to rage that devastated all around.
Pelops, beloved son of Tantalus,
Acquired a wife through treachery and murder.
The sons of Pelops, one of them called Atreus,
Were bent on fratricide. The son of Atreus
Was Agamemnon. His wife was Clytemnestra,
Who bore first me, Electra next,
And finally Orestes, our brother.
My father reigned in peace, the perfect model
Of a man. The curse on Tantalus
Seemed laid to rest. Then came the Trojan War.
My father led the army sent to rescue Helen.
Diana, angered by my father, held back the fleet,
Demanding my life in sacrifice to let it sail.
The Greeks agreed. Diana didn't spill
My blood, but spirited me away.
Here in this temple I found my life restored.
I, who speak to you, descend from Atreus,

I'm Agamemnon's daughter.
I am bound to serve Diana.

Thoas: In you as daughter of a king I place
No greater store than in the trusted stranger.
What I have proposed I now repeat:
Come, follow me and share in all I have.

Iphigenie: O King, how can I dare accept?
Saved by the goddess, Diana,
I consecrate my life to her.
She found me refuge. Perhaps she plans,
Her anger with my father satisfied,
To bring me back to him, a joy in his old age.
What if this is meant to happen soon,
And I, against her will, am bound to you?
I need her sign if I am to remain.

Thoas: You are still here. That's sign enough.
Anxiety is making you evasive.
In vain with words you try to cloud the issue.
The only word I hear is "no".

Iphigenie: My words I use not to disguise
But to reveal to you my deepest thoughts.
And you yourself appreciate the longing
That draws me, anxious, to my home,
To the halls where sadness speaks my name in whispers.
Joy, as for a new-born child, will perhaps one day ring out.
Your ships could bring me home!
This would bring both me and mine to life!

Thoas: Then go. Go back. Just listen to your heart,
Ignore what wisdom and good sense dictate.
Act like a woman! Surrender to this craze!
Out of control, swing rudderless this way and that!
Desire of any kind, once entering a woman's breast,
Will loose her from the faithful, proven love
Of father, husband. For her no bond is sacred.
And even when this rapid flame dies down,
The golden words of truth and loyalty,
However powerfully expressed,
Make no impression.

Iphigenie: Thoas, recall your noble word.
Is this your answer? You were disposed to
Listen to whatever I would say.

Thoas: I was not prepared for such unwelcome words.
But then I should have been: for, after all,
From a woman what can one expect?

Iphigenie: Our sex does not deserve rebuke.
Our weapons are less glorious than yours,
However, not less noble. In fact,
What's good for you I understand
Far better than you do yourself.
You are in tune so little with yourself
And me and yet you think a closer bond
Will bring us happiness together.
With good intentions, the best will in the world,
You press me to agree with you.
But here I thank the gods: they strengthen me.
This union, of which they disapprove,
I don't accept.

Thoas: The gods! This disapproval is spoken by your heart.

Iphigenie: The heart! That's where their words are to be heard.

Thoas: Have I no right to hear their words as well?

Iphigenie: The raging storm drowns out their gentle tones.

Thoas: The priestess, of course, is the only one who hears.

Iphigenie: The ruler should be the first to listen.

Thoas: Your sacred office, the right you have inherited
To sit at table with the gods
Exalts *you* over earthlings like myself!

Iphigenie: This is how I pay for opening my
Heart as you demanded.

Thoas: I'm only human. We've talked enough.
Here's my final word: *be* Diana's priestess,
Since she has chosen you. I pray she will forgive me
That I have wrongly and against my inner voice
Deprived her of her sacrificial victims.
It is our ancient custom: certain death
Awaits whoever as a stranger nears our shores.
You alone, with all your charm,
In which I sometimes saw a loving daughter
And sometimes the sweet affection of a bride,
Have tied my hands and made me shirk my duty.
You made me deaf: and now the people's voice,
Which I ignored, is loud in blaming me
For my son's untimely death.
I will no longer, just for you,
Restrain the crowd when they insist on sacrifice.

Iphigenie: Just for me? No! Restrain them for the gods.
Bloodthirsty desires of men, their savage deeds
Are not the gods' responsibility.
Did not Diana, herself a goddess,
Save me from the sacrificial knife,
To have me serve her rather than to die?

Thoas: It's not our place, with subtle reason,
To interpret sacred practice according to our whims.
Do your duty, as I do mine.
I have in custody two strangers
Found hiding by the shore. They have some plot.
Let these be offered to Diana
As sacrificial victims - her first, long overdue.
I'll send them here. You know what you've to do.

Scene Four

Iphigenie alone.

Iphigenie: Gracious Diana, you have clouds, you have winds
To spirit away the victims of oppression,
And carry them across the widest stretch of sea and land
To the haven of your choice.
You are wise, you see into the future.
The past has not escaped you.
Your gaze shines on your servants
As your light, the moon, reigns over earth at night
Radiating life and calm.
Don't sully my hands with blood
Which never brings blessing or peace.
The face of the murdered victim
Will haunt in horrible nightmares
The unwilling perpetrator of the deed.

The gods, in love and goodwill, embrace
The far-flung tribes of men and gladly
Give them life to share, if only in a glimpse,
The bliss the gods themselves enjoy eternally.

ACT TWO

Scene One

Orestes and Pylades.

Orestes: Our every step leads only to our death
And inwardly I feel at peace.
I begged Apollo to rid me of these vengeful spirits.
He seemed to promise help, security
In the temple of his much beloved sister
Who reigns in Tauris. His words were spoken
Full of hope, divine in their assurance.
But now it seems deliverance lies in death.
It's no great sorrow to bid farewell
To the sun's bright light. My heart is
Crushed by the gods, my senses dulled.
My forefathers died, not victorious in battle
But like sacrificial animals. I, too,
Am better off to die before the altar
Than to be trapped by my kin in their murderous nets.
But meantime, leave me peace, you spirits from below.
The blood upon my path attracts you here.
There's time enough. The light of day is not for you
Nor me, the earth's green sward no place
For shadows' play. Down there I'll find you,
Down there we'll share the grim eternal night.
My Pylades, companion – though innocent –

Of my guilt and my disgrace: my only sadness is
That you, so young, must share my fate.
To think of you alive or dead
Inspires me with hope or dread.

Pylades: I'm not like you, Orestes, prepared
To sink into that world of shadows.
These tangled winding paths
Which seem to lead to death
Could lead us back to life.
My mind is not on death. I'm listening
To the counsel of the gods. Perhaps
They plan for us a route for our escape.
Whether feared or not, death cannot be stopped,
But even when the priestess, in consecrating
Us to death, raises her hand
To cut our locks of hair, not death
But life for us will occupy my mind.
Raise yourself above our plight.
Despair will only hasten death.
Apollo gave his word: his sister's temple
Is your source of consolation, aid,
An avenue of escape. The words of gods
Are not ambiguous. Your depression makes them so.

Orestes: My mother cast this shadow over me,
A tender child. I was the image of my father.
My silent gaze, as I grew up, she read
As a reproach. She had a lover.
When Electra, my sister, sat in silence
At the hearth in the spacious hall
I sat anxious in her lap, and as she wept
Her bitter tears, I stared into her face.
She then spoke much of father's noble deeds.
I longed to see him, to be at his side.

I wanted for myself to be in Troy,
For him to be at home.
Then came the day –

Pylades: Let the dead converse about that hour!
The memory of better times should strengthen
Our resolve to serve the needs of this wide earth.
The gods have need of you – not as companion
To your father, who went, unwilling, to his death.

Orestes: I wish I'd clung to him and followed him.

Pylades: But those who offered you protection
Were my support as well. Had we not shared
Our lives, where would I be? Since childhood
My life has been with you, was yours.

Orestes: Those days of happiness – please don't remind me.
Your house and family had made me free.
Your noble father, a wise and kindly man,
Watched over my growth in those delicate years,
And you, my ever cheerful friend, were in my life
Each day, a bright butterfly around a sombre flower.
Your joy poured into me and I forgot my cares,
This tide of youth swept both of us away.

Pylades: This was, for me, the time when life began.

Orestes: Or, better said: when trouble began.
I'm like an outcast, like a plague. A hidden sorrow,
Death itself is in me. It disturbs me that,
Wherever I encounter health and life,
Through me the joyful faces are soon
Lined with pain, oncoming death.

Pylades: If this is what you cause,
Should I not be the first to wither, die?
How has your breath not blighted me?
You see my openness, I still have joy for living.
And joy and love can inspire in us great deeds.

Orestes: Great deeds? There was a time we thought of that.
Up hill, down dale we charged together, hunting.
Our hopes were high one day to imitate
Our noble fathers. We puffed our chests
And raised our fists. We'd use both club and sword
To vanquish monsters; we'd track down robbers.
The evenings saw us sitting by the lakes,
Propped one against the other, the waves were
Lapping at our feet. The world seemed wide,
It seemed to beckon us. With hand on sword
We dreamed heroic deeds unnumbered as the stars.
And yet, since then the gods have made of me a butcher.
I've put to death the mother I revered -
One shameful act avenged by yet another.
It's clear, the gods have planned the downfall
Of our house, and I, the last in line,
Am destined for disgrace and shame.

Pylades: The gods don't blame our fathers' sins on us.
Rewards will correspond to deeds.
Our parents' blessing, not their curse
Is our inheritance.

Orestes: I wouldn't say their blessing led us here!

Pylades: No doubt the gods have formed their own design.

Orestes: If so, they're bent on our destruction.

Pylades: Do what they command and bide your time.
Apollo wants the image of his sister
Brought to him in Delphi. There, the gods
Both honoured by their people, will in return,
Reward your deed and rescue you from danger.
Already in this sacred grove they've made you safe.

Orestes: They're making sure I have a peaceful death.

Pylades: That's not my view of things. My hunch –
And it's a good one – tells me past events
Are not without a future. The gods' great plan
Has perhaps long since been formed. Diana
Longs to quit the shores of these
Barbarians and their human sacrifice.
We are her chosen agents. The strangest means
Have brought us to her portals.

Orestes: The gods' design fits nicely with your wishes.

Pylades: You think it's too far-fetched? I've chatted
With our guards. I know from them
There is a woman, a stranger, half like a goddess,
Who keeps the savage custom in abeyance.
She brings the gods not human sacrifice
But purity of heart, and incense and prayer.
She's held in high esteem. They think
She is of Amazon descent, that she has fled
When threatened by some great calamity.

Orestes: It seems the light she sheds is dimmed.
The presence of a criminal is too much.
The curse that follows him brings night
To all around. Desire for blood awakes
The sacred custom to destroy us.

The savage King is bent on death for us.
What can a woman do when he's enraged?

Pylades: Be grateful it's a woman. A man,
However good, gets used to cruelty.
What initially disgusts him will end up
As a law. When steeled by habit,
He soon becomes a mask.
Constancy is only found in women.
For good or ill you can rely on them.
But, quiet! Look, she's coming!
Leave me alone with her.
I must conceal our names and not confide
Our story openly. Go now.
I'll meet you before you talk with her. *Exit Orestes.*

Scene Two

Enter Iphigenie.

Iphigenie: Tell me, stranger, where you come from.
It seems to me you could be Greek.
You're hardly from a Scythian land.
She removes his chains.
Freedom I give you, but not from peril.
May the gods avert whatever danger threatens.

Pylades: Your voice is sweet to hear.
My mother tongue, a welcome sound
In this strange land, calls up for me, a prisoner,
The vision of the azure mountains that surround
Our native harbour. You see my joy!
Let it convince you that I, like you, am Greek.
Distracted by that splendid vision,

An instant I forgot my need of you.
Please tell me, unless some sacred law
Has sealed your lips, the godlike line of your descent.

Iphigenie: That I am priestess of Diana,
Chosen and consecrated by her hand,
Is all you need to know. Tell me who you are.
What wretched, irresistible destiny has driven
You and your companion to these shores?

Pylades: We come from Crete. I am Cephalus.
He is Laodamas, my brother. He slew our other
Brother – a dispute about the booty my father
Brought from Troy. Laodamas is crazed with guilt.
Apollo sent us to these savage shores
To find his sister's temple and here await
Diana's help and solace. The rest you know:
As captives we've been brought to you -
Sacrificial victims.

Iphigenie: You mentioned Troy. Tell me: it must have fallen!

Pylades: It did. But guarantee us safety. Give speedily
The help the gods have promised. Take pity
On my brother and heal him with your words.
I beg you, when you speak to him, be gentle,
Kindly. Joy and pain – and even memory –
Can take over and devastate his soul.
His inner harmony is torn with fits of madness
And remorse.

Iphigenie: But Troy! – I see your plight –
First speak to me of Troy!

Pylades: That great city, for ten long years
The Greeks could not subdue. But now
It lies in rubble. It will never rise again.
Yet Troy remains, the graveyard of our men,
Imprinted in our minds. Achilles and his friend...

Iphigenie: Are dead? These godlike men are dust?

Pylades: Palamedes and Ajax lie there too.

Iphigenie: Aside No mention of my father.
He's not among the dead! I'll see him!
Dare I hope?

Pylades: The fate of all
Who died in this campaign was bitter-sweet.
But one man who survived, returning home victorious,
Was greeted, not in triumph, but with horrors
Planned for him by angry gods.
You haven't heard? Reports of his sad fate
Are known throughout the world. You didn't know
What sorrow, because of these atrocious deeds,
Fills that family's house with sighs? Clytemnestra,
Aided by Aegisthus, ensnared her husband,
The day of his return from Troy. They murdered him. –
I see you hold this family in high esteem.
Your bosom heaves, this unexpected, monstrous news...
Are you the daughter of his friend? Perhaps a neighbour?
Speak openly. Forgive me. It's my misfortune
That you heard it first through me.

Iphigenie: Describe it to me now,
Exactly as it happened.

Pylades: The day of his arrival home
The King, refreshed, relaxing in his bath,
Asked Clytemnestra for his clothes.
Instead, she threw a treacherous net, with many folds,
Around his head and shoulders, and as he strove
In vain to extricate himself, Aegisthus, his betrayer,
Struck and sent him to his grave.

Iphigenie: And how was Aegisthus rewarded for his deed?

Pylades: With a kingdom and a bed. But these
Were long since his.

Iphigenie: The motive for this crime was lust?

Pylades: But also his wife's desire for revenge.

Iphigenie: Why? What injury had he done her?

Pylades: A deed so grievous, that, if murder
Could ever be condoned, this would condone it.
Unfavourable winds delayed the Greeks from sailing
Off to Troy. The angry goddess, Diana, was
Holding up his fleet. Appeasing her,
The King enticed his eldest daughter, Iphigenie
To Aulis, where in sacrifice he slaughtered her –
All in the cause of Greece. So Clytemnestra,
In outrage, responded to Aegisthus' overtures
And together they brought about his death.

Iphigenie: (*turning aside*) I've heard enough. We'll talk again.
Exit.

Pylades: The story of this regal family has deeply moved her.
No doubt she knew the King and is herself

Of noble birth, sold – in marriage? – to someone here.
It's our good fortune. A glimmer of hope appears.
Cautious, courageous, let's go to meet it.

ACT THREE

Scene One

Iphigenie and Orestes.

Iphigenie: I set you free, but only of these chains.
It is a sign, like the last glimpse of sunlight
To a dying man, that outside this temple
Death awaits you. And so you're lost?
That's not for me to say. But if you die,
It won't be by *my* hand. As long as I am
Priestess of Diana, no one, no matter
Who he is, can do you any harm.
And yet, if I reject the angered King's demands
He'll put another in my place, and then
What can I offer you? My good-will!...
You are my countryman. To any Greek,
No matter what his status, I've spoken
Words of welcome in this foreign land.
How joyful, full of blessing should be my words of
Welcome to men who conjure up for me
The image of the heroes I learned from childhood
To revere. Through you I have new hope,
My heart stirs in me again.

Orestes: Is there some reason you conceal
Your name and origin? You're like a goddess.

Will you tell me who you are?.

Iphigenie: I'll tell you in good time. But meanwhile,
Finish the story your brother had begun.
What happened to those who, coming home from Troy,
Found on their threshold a bitter shock awaiting them?
I came here young, but I remember how,
With looks of fear and admiration
I gazed upon these men. They marched away
As if divinely sent to emulate their forbears' deeds.
They would strike terror into Trojan hearts.
Most glorious of all was Agamemnon.
A victim, was he, on his arrival home,
Of Clytemnestra and Aegisthus' treachery?

Orestes: He was.

Iphigenie: Catastrophe! My wretched homeland!
Sown with curse upon curse by the wild progeny
Of Tantalus. Like weeds that shake their heads
And strew their thousand seeds to every wind,
They generate a race that murders kith and kin.
The curse lives on, perpetuates itself. -
And now, reveal to me the things black fear forbade
Me ask your brother: Orestes, the lovely child,
The last boy of this illustrious line, set aside
To avenge his slaughtered father,
What news of him? Did he survive that bloody day?
He managed to escape? He's still alive? Electra too?

Orestes: They are alive.

Iphigenie: O may the golden sun lend me its beauteous rays
That I may offer them in thanks to Jupiter.
I have no gifts, no words.

Orestes: If friendship or a closer bond unites you
With this regal house – your joy tells me it does –
Then brace yourself: to fall headlong from joy
To sorrow is unbearable. You know
Of Agamemnon's death? That's all?

Iphigenie: That's all! To me it seems enough.

Orestes: You've only heard the half.

Iphigenie: What else is there to fear? You said
Orestes and Electra are still alive.

Orestes: You have no fears for Clytemnestra?

Iphigenie: Fears or hopes – what good are they to *her*?

Orestes: She's parted from the land of hope.

Iphigenie: Her own blood she spilled in violent remorse?

Orestes: Her own blood it was that killed her.

Iphigenie: Don't speak in riddles. My mind is riven
With uncertainties. I need to know the truth.

Orestes: And so the gods have chosen me as messenger.
I must relate a deed I would rather have consigned
To the hollow, voiceless realms of darkness.
Your lovely lips compel me against my will.
Your voice alone, though courting sorrow, can make
Demands of me and have them met.
The day her father fell, Electra saved Orestes.
Concealing him, she put him in her uncle's care.

Along with Pylades, his son, he reared Orestes.
The closest bonds were formed between the boys.
As they grew up, within them grew a raging fire
That devoured them with thoughts of vengeance
For the King. Then one day, unannounced,
Disguised in foreign clothes, they came with
News: Orestes was dead. They'd brought his ashes.
From Clytemnestra they receive a welcome,
They're brought into the house. Electra,
When told it is her brother, excites in him
The fierce fires of revenge which in his mother's
Sacred presence have died down.
She leads him quietly to the place his father fell.
The faintest streaks of blood, despite repeated cleansing,
Do not escape the eye. Like spitting fire, her tongue
Describes the shameful deed - no detail spared - ,
And then the wretched servant's life she's led,
The arrogant behaviour of the killers,
The dangers to which the young ones are exposed
Now that their mother is estranged.
Electra places in his hand the ancient dagger
That wrought havoc in the house of Tantalus.
Now Clytemnestra falls, the victim of her son.

Iphigenie: Immortal gods! You live in bliss
Surrounded every day by new and fresher clouds.
You isolated me so many years and kept
Me to yourselves, entrusted me with tending
The holy flame. Like it, my soul ascends
To your eternal realms and seeks your light.
You wanted to conceal from me my family's fate,
That I should suffer more by learning of it late? –
Now tell me, what concerns me most,
Tell me of Orestes' tragic lot.

Orestes: If only I could tell you he was dead!
His slaughtered mother's spirit rose up as if
Fermenting with her blood and cried:
"Don't let this matricide escape. Track down
The criminal, and he is yours."
The avenging furies looked up and listened
Where they lurked in black hollows, the greed of eagles
In their eyes. Their allies, remorse and doubt,
Were quickly at their side. A sudden mist arising
From the underworld engulfed his guilty head,
Confusing him with thoughts unending
Of his dire deed. And they, in justified destruction,
Now trod the earth they once had been forbidden by
A curse. They tracked the fugitive in hot pursuit,
Allowed him rest which then they filled with horror.

Iphigenie: Poor man, your story is the same.
You feel the persecution you describe.

Orestes: What's this you say? My story is the same?

Iphigenie: The weight of such a death as this, a fratricide,
Oppresses you – your youngest brother
Has confided it to me.

Orestes: I cannot bear to see a woman such as you
Deceived. A web of lies is spread by men –
For men well used to traps and guile.
But you must hear the truth from me.
Orestes? – I am Orestes! My head, guilt-laden,
Is bowed down to the grave in search
Of death – whatever form it takes.
For you, whoever you may be, and for my friend,
I wish a speedy rescue – not for myself.
I feel you're living here against your will.

You both should plan for your escape,
But not with me. Lifeless, my corpse may
Hurtle down a cliff, my steaming blood may flow
Into the sea and bring its curse to these
Barbaric shores. But you, go back to Greece.
At home you may begin your life anew.
He moves away.

Iphigenie: At last, the words I've waited for!
Remote from me your secret plans,
Your gifts held back in wisdom
From child-like, outstretched hands
Until you saw the time was ripe.
You never pick the fruit before its time,
And woe to those who'd snatch it unripe
From the tree. But let not the long awaited,
Half-forgotten moment of fulfilment
Flit by in vain, and, passing
Like the ghost of a departed friend,
Leave greater sorrow than I ever knew before.

Orestes: *Approaching her.*
If you are calling on the gods for you
And Pylades, leave out my name.
The criminal cannot be saved.
Don't ally yourself with me, my flight and fate.

Iphigenie: Your fate and mine are closely intertwined.

Orestes: That cannot be. My death is mine and mine alone.
Your veil around me could not conceal my guilt.
The baleful eyes would find me out.
Your presence, holy as it is, can fend them off,
But they are there. They may not tread this holy ground,
Yet now and then I hear the menace

Of their laughter. They bay like wolves
Beneath the tree a traveller has climbed for refuge.
Out there they lie in wait, and once I leave the grove
They will arise in clouds of dust, and, shaking
Serpent heads, they'll track their fleeing prey.

Iphigenie: Orestes, do you have an ear for friendly words?

Orestes: Save them up for some friend of the gods.

Iphigenie: They offer you a ray of hope.

Orestes: Through smoke and gloom I see the grim
Reflection of the river Styx that points me
To my death.

Iphigenie: Electra you mentioned. Is she your only sister?

Orestes: The only one I knew. The elder had a better fate –
Which at the time seemed worse – that saved
Her from our family's catastrophic plight.
But now, drop the questions. The furies ask enough.
They keep alive the coals of memory
That burn in me. My mind is branded,
Seared with the tortures the gods thought up for us.

Iphigenie: I bring the scent of incense to this flame.
The breath of love will cool the fire raging
In your bosom. My dear Orestes, do you not hear?
Has your persecution by the furies so
Arrested the flow of blood within your veins?
The ugly Gorgon's gaze has turned your limbs
To stone? Well, if the voice of mother's
Blood, when spilled, can reach far down to hell itself,
Can not a sister, favoured of the gods,

Call down a blessing from on high?

Orestes: That voice, that voice! It calls for my destruction!
Are you an avenging fury in disguise?
Who are you, who incite this raging turmoil
Deep inside me?

Iphigenie: The deepest regions of your heart announce it:
Orestes, it's me. I'm Iphigenie,
Alive before your eyes!

Orestes: You!

Iphigenie: My brother!

Orestes: Don't! Get back! Be warned!
The raging fire the furies fan in me
Will leap at you for your destruction. Begone!
I'll face my shameful death in isolation.

Iphigenie: You will not die. One quiet word
From you will wipe away my doubts.
Confirm for me: the hour of bliss I've yearned for
These many years has now arrived.
Inside me spins a wheel of joy and pain.
I shrink from you when you appear a stranger.
A violent urge within me drives me to embrace
In you my brother.

Orestes: Whose temple do you serve? Whose priestess here
Is gripped with such a frenzied rage?
A nymph for my seduction?
How can I trust you and all your flattery?
The servants of Diana are much stricter.
The desecration of her temple won't go unpunished.

Your hands! – keep them away from me!
You want to save a young man with your love?
You have such tenderness and joy to offer?
Then give them to a worthier man: my friend.
You'll find him on a path among the rocks out there.
Lead him along – then leave me alone.

Iphigenie: Orestes, look! I am your sister!
Mine is a sister's joy, unspeakable –
Not some lawless passion. –
Oh, give him eyes to see. From exaltation
In this moment we could plummet to despair. –
The sister long since snatched from you
Stands right before your eyes. The goddess
Saved me, brought me to her temple here.
You are a captive, to be offered up in sacrifice.
The priestess appointed to perform this rite is
None other than your sister!

Orestes: None better! Bring on Electra to be destroyed
With us instead of living out her wretched life.
Fine, priestess! Show me the altar.
Fratricide is part of our inheritance.
I thank the gods: they have decreed
My death before they gave me children.
And you, take my advice. Forget the sun,
Forget the stars. Come down with me.
The darker world awaits us.
Our race, like dragons bred in smoke and fire,
Devours its flesh and blood.
You have no children. You have your innocence.
Come down with me before it is too late.
You look at me with pity in your eyes. No use!
With eyes like that your mother searched my heart.
It didn't stop the blow I struck her breast.

She fell. It's now her turn. You too, avenging furies,
Gather round. Enjoy with her this welcome
Spectacle, the last, the cruellest for our race.
Not hatred, not revenge prepares the knife.
My loving sister must needs perform the deed.
No tears! It's not your fault. Since tender
Childhood years there's no one I have loved
Like you, beloved sister. Now, wield your blade
And don't hold back. My heart, cut open,
Will release the streams of seething blood.
He collapses, unconscious.

Iphigenie: Too much for one alone this joy, this grief. –
Where are you? I need your help, good Pylades.
She goes off in search of him.

Scene Two

Orestes alone.

Orestes: *Regains consciousness and sits up.*
Another cup! Pass me, from the waters of
Oblivion, the final cool refreshing drink
To wash away the cramping strains of life.
My mind, adrift on this forgetful tide,
Slips quietly into eternal mists. In darkness
Let me find elusive rest.
These whispering voices amongst the leaves!
Is this a princely throng that comes to
Greet me? Old and young, men and women,
They look like gods, resembling one another.
I bid you welcome, I, with whom your dynasty
Becomes extinct. What you have sown,
Orestes reaps. My father, is it you?

Is this my mother at your side?
If Clytemnestra is allowed to take your hand,
Then I, Orestes, can approach her saying:
"I am your son!" Look both of you upon your son
And welcome him. The presence of a murderer
In our midst is nothing new. Present me now
To Tantalus, our ancestor. I long
To contemplate his features, the honoured man
Who sat at table with the gods. You hesitate?
You turn away? In sorrow? It cannot be!
This demi-god is laden down with chains,
A prey to cruel tortures.

Scene Three

Enter Iphigenie and Pylades.

Orestes: You too have come? So soon?
My sister, welcome! We only need Electra now.
Perhaps a god with kindly, gentle means
Will quickly send her down to us.
My friend – for you I do regret…
But come, come both of you, as guests,
To meet the god who rules this dark domain.

Iphigenie: Apollo, Diana, brother and sister,
You shed your light on us by day and night
But do not reach the regions of the dead.
Diana, you love your brother, you turn
Your virgin face with longing towards his light:
Don't let my brother, just found, be lost
In these dark ravings. You planned,
In sheltering me here, to bring me help
Through him and bring him peace through me.

Release him from the shackles of this curse
In case this precious chance should slip away.

Pylades: You know us, Orestes, and this holy grove,
You know the light that shines on us and not the dead.
You feel the arm of friend and sister
Grip you tight. Take hold of us, alive.
In us you have no empty shadows.
You hear my voice: now listen. Pull yourself together.
Our rescue is hanging from a thread
Spun graciously for us, and yet at any moment
We could see it cut.

Orestes: *to Iphigenie.*
My sister, in your embrace my heart will know
Its purest joy. The gods, whose all-consuming power
Dries up the clouds, announces with thund'rous voice
And booming storms the advent of the
Longed for showers of rain – these gods
Can turn a dreaded fate, an awesome prospect
Into a blessing, a rainbow,
That draws from us a prayer of thanks.
Grant me, in my sister's arms, my friend's embrace,
To enjoy in gratitude, secure, what you bestow:
The curse, my heart tells me, is lifted.
I hear the furies leaving for the underworld.
I hear, like distant thunder, the iron gates of hell
Slam closed behind them. Refreshed, the earth invites me
To its pastures, its joy, its vibrant activity.

Pylades: Orestes! Our time is strictly measured.
Our joy will be the breeze that fills our sails
Let's now discuss our plans and make decisions.

ACT FOUR

Scene One

Iphigenie alone.

Iphigenie: I see in Pylades a strong young man in battle,
A wise old head in conference.
His inner poise brings guidance, stability
When otherwise confusion reigns. He tore me
From my brother's arms. In my astonishment
I'd clung to him, oblivious of danger,
And now, to carry out their plan, they've left me here
And gone to find the ship, obscured in
A bay where friends are waiting for a sign.
They've told me what to say to Thoas when
He orders me to carry out the sacrifice.
They have to treat me like a child. Deceit,
Its devious arts I've never learned. I fear
That falsehood is a shaft that wounds
Both victim and the marksman. Where openness
Should liberate, I feel constricted by this mounting
Fear. Perhaps the furies, outside this consecrated
Ground, will persecute Orestes yet again. –
I hear armed men approaching. Are they discovered?
The messenger from Thoas is arriving here in haste.
My heart is pounding. How false it feels
To face this man with nothing but a web of lies.

Scene Two

Enter Arkas.

Arkas: Priestess, proceed to carry out the sacrifice.
The King is waiting. The people are impatient.

Iphigenie: My duty and your wishes I would have carried out
But for an unexpected hindrance.

Arkas: What sort of hindrance can thwart the King's command?

Iphigenie: Chance and fortune, over which there's no control.

Arkas: Explain it. The King must know at once,
For he's decided that both the men must die.

Iphigenie: The gods themselves are far less hasty.
The elder of these men has spilled the blood
Of nearest kin. For this the furies hound him.
This holy place has witnessed their attack,
Thus desecration of the temple has occurred.
I now must hurry with my servants to the sea
To bathe Diana's statue in the waves.
No one must disturb us as we carry out
These rites of consecration

Arkas: I will report this to the King without delay.
You must await from him permission to proceed.

Iphigenie: This is a matter for the priestess to decide.

Arkas: The case is strange. The King must be informed.

Iphigenie: His advice, as his command, can alter nothing.

Arkas: You must at least appear to ask the King.

Iphigenie: Do not demand what can but be refused.

Arkas: Do not refuse demands both good and fitting.

Iphigenie: Should there be no delay, then I agree.

Arkas: I'll hurry with this message to his quarters
And soon relay his answer back to you.
There *is* a message I could bring to him,
And then the problem would be solved.
You paid no heed to my well-meant advice.

Iphigenie: I've gladly done whatever I could do.

Arkas: You'll change your mind while there's still time.

Iphigenie: Is not such change at times beyond our power?

Arkas: Beyond our power? You mean, not worth the effort?

Iphigenie: And you can change according to your wish?

Arkas: And you are so serene in courting danger?

Iphigenie: My faith is in the gods and them alone.

Arkas: They find solutions using human means.

Iphigenie: They give us signs we are obliged to follow.

Arkas: I tell you, the solution rests with you. Because
The King is angry he demands the strangers' death.

The army's finished with this brutal sacrifice,
This unnecessary bloodshed. You introduced us
To a mild regime. You can confirm us in it.
Our people, young and wild, are full of strength,
But, leave them to themselves, they feel unstable,
Insecure. You know they look to you.

Iphigenie: Twist my heart within me. You'll never change my mind.

Arkas: While there's still time no effort should be spared,
And healing, helpful words must still be spoken.

Iphigenie: Your efforts and the pain you cause me
Are both in vain. It's better that you go.

Arkas: You're wrong. The pain I cause you is my ally.
It points you in the right direction.

Iphigenie: The violence it does me cannot make me budge.

Arkas: And so you baulk at such a noble gesture?

Iphigenie: Yes, when the noble man expects of me
The wrong response and not my thanks.

Arkas: Where there's no feeling there's never lack of words.
I'll tell the King of your response. It's clear
You don't recall his graciousness to you
Since your arrival on these shores.

Scene Three

Iphigenie alone.

Iphigenie: His words have caused upheaval in my heart.
As swiftly flowing water conceals the jagged
Rocks that lurk within the sandy banks,
A flood of joy obscured my inner self.
In my arms I held the longed for prize.
It seemed impossible, as if another cloud
Had settled gently round me for my rescue,
Diana wafting me away as in a dream.
My heart had seized with violence upon my brother.
I had ears for nothing but his friend's advice.
My one desire had been to save them both.
This craggy island, Tauris, already lay behind me.
But all at once the dream was shattered by
This good man's voice reminding me
What friends I would abandon here. Deceit
I hate, now doubly so. Be calm. You waver?
You begin to doubt? If you allow yourself
To go adrift you'll lose all focus – within
Yourself and in the world around you.

Scene Four

Enter Pylades.

Pylades: Where is she? She must hear at once about
Our rescue.

Iphigenie: I'm waiting, worried. Your news,
I trust, has brought me consolation

Pylades: Orestes is healed! Lightheartedly we left
The grove behind us and walked across the rocks
And sands, unconsecrated ground – and nothing happened!
The joy of youth returned to him. His gleaming eye
Showed courage, hope. His heart was free again,
His mind preoccupied alone with thoughts of saving
You, his rescuer, and me, his friend.

Iphigenie: May your lips be blessed for speaking words
Like these, and may they never have to utter
Sounds of suffering and lamentation.

Pylades: There's more good news, for happiness,
Just like a prince, is well escorted. We found
Our companions grimly waiting in a cove
Where they'd concealed the ship. They saw
Your brother, were exultant, but then insisted
That we all depart without delay.
Their hands were itching to take the oars
And, as they soon became aware, a gentle
Breeze had risen. So now, let's hurry.
Bring me to the temple, let me enter,
Attain the goal that brought us here.
Unaided I can shoulder the statue of Diana,
A burden I've long desired to bear.
*He goes towards the temple as he speaks these last words without noticing
that Iphigenie does not follow him. Eventually he turns round.*
You stand there, hesitating – tell me – you're silent.
You seem confused. Is there another problem
To confront? You *did* relay our message
To the King as we agreed?

Iphigenie: I did, good friend, and yet I see
Myself exposed to your reproach. I spoke
With Arkas exactly as you said. He seemed

Amazed and then became insistent: the King
Must hear of this unusual ceremony and give
Consent. He's gone to Thoas. I'm awaiting
His return.

Pylades: But that's disastrous news! It means
Fresh dangers hanging over us. The priestess
Has a right to veil the truth. What have you done?!

Iphigenie: As priestess I've never tried to veil the truth.

Pylades: You are so innocent and pure that you'll
Destroy yourself and us. I should have guessed
He'd make demands like this and told you
What to say.

Iphigenie: Your reproach, I know, is justified,
But what else could I do, what answer could
I give the man whose words, so wise and good,
Were echoed in my heart?

Pylades: The noose is tightening around us.
But, even now, hold firm and think. Do nothing
Rash. Await the messenger's return.
Then stand your ground, whatever he reports.
The celebration of such rites is matter
For the priestess, not the King. And if
He asks to see the stranger, the victim of
The curse, you just refuse, pretending you
Are holding both of us as prisoners
In the temple. This paves the way for us
In haste to wrest the holy statue – and ourselves -
From these unworthy, barbarian hands.
The clearest signs are shown us by Apollo:
Though we, as yet, have not fulfilled his one

Condition, he has already, godlike, fulfilled
His solemn promise. Orestes is liberated, cured.
May favourable winds bring us and him
To where Apollo dwells – that island of rocks
And cliffs – then home. Mycena,
Beckons us. We'll bring it life. The dying
Embers of each hearth will glow, burst
Into flames and brighten with their light
Each dwelling place. Your role will be,
Atoning for the curse, to scatter incense
Everywhere, restoring to your family
Its joy for living.

Iphigenie: Your words, my friend, turn me like a flower
Towards the sun. Without a voice like this,
Without this reassuring presence, I could
Sink into myself. Where thought, decision
In isolation ripen all too slowly,
A loving presence will quickly make them grow.

Pylades: But now, goodbye. I must return. Our friends
Are waiting anxiously for news. When I
Come back I'll wait amongst these bushes for
A sign from you – what's wrong? What's on your mind?
A sudden look of sadness has come over you.

Iphigenie: I'm sorry. Like a wisp of cloud that drifts
Before the sun a momentary worry
Has dulled my joy.

Pylades: Don't be alarmed. It's clear that fear and danger
Form a close alliance.

Iphigenie: And yet my worry cannot lightly
Be dismissed. It warns me not to rob,

Not to deceive the King, my second father.

Pylades: You flee the man who plans to kill your brother.

Iphigenie: This very man did only good to me.

Pylades: You *have* to flee – that's not ingratitude!

Iphigenie: It remains ingratitude. My plight is my excuse.

Pylades: Both gods and men will find it valid.

Iphigenie: I cannot solve the conflict in myself.

Pylades: Your hidden pride dictates this stern demand.

Iphigenie: There's no demand. I'm saying what I feel.

Pylades: You must feel proud to have so fine a conscience.

Iphigenie: Integrity alone can give us inner peace.

Pylades: It's just as well you're living in a temple.
Life teaches us a different lesson – to be
Less strict with others and ourselves. You'll
Learn this, too. The lives of human beings
Are so entangled, so intertwined that none
Can find such inner peace within himself
Nor live in harmony with all around.
We're not appointed to pass judgement on
Ourselves. We go our way, we watch our step –
That's all we can be asked to do. We seldom
Judge correctly what we've done, still less
Can we interpret what we're doing.

Iphigenie: I must admit, your argument's persuasive.

Pylades: Persuasive! When you know there is no choice?
There's just one way to save yourself, your brother
And a friend – why would you need persuasion?

Iphigenie: You understand my hesitation. If you
Yourself felt deepest obligation to a man
You would hesitate to do him such injustice.

Pylades: You're facing bitterest reproach if we
Are all condemned, and deep despair. It's clear
That compromise is new to you. However
Dire the consequence, you cannot bend
The truth?

Iphigenie: I'd need to be a man, for men
Are deaf to all that hinders their great plans.

Pylades: There's no point in your resistance. Necessity
Dictates to you, and even to the gods.
It indicates the path you are to follow.
When it silently commands, you must
Obey. You know the rest. I'll soon be back
Receiving from your sacred hands the statue
Of Diana to guarantee our rescue.

Scene Five

Iphigenie alone.

I have to yield, since danger to Orestes
And his friend is imminent. And yet
I have this growing fear of what the future

Holds for me. The silent hope I cherished
In my loneliness is to be extinguished
By this never-ending curse? Can no blessing
Bring this family new life? But surely
Everything must have an end. Our highest
Joys, the vigour of our lives, they all
Begin to fade. Why not the curse as well?
It seems my hopes were vain. I was removed,
Protected here from sharing in my loved
Ones' fate. My role was to atone for guilt
By innocence, for slaughter by giving life
And love - and finally purify my father's
House. When in an instant my brother
In my embrace escapes at last the haunting
Curse, the very moment the longed-for ship
Approaches with promise of my returning home,
The cold hand of necessity demands
Of me a double crime: to steal the honoured
Statue entrusted to my care and to
Betray the man who saved my life and saved
Me from my fate. Could hatred now, with vultures'
Claws, possess my tender breast? Could I
Be tempted like my Titan forbears, to
Rise up, rebellious against you, Olympian gods?
Save me, and if in me you see your image,
Save yourselves. I hear the echo of
The chilling song I'd long forgotten – and
How gladly I'd forgotten! When Tantalus fell,
Rejected by the gods, the fates, in grim
Compassion for their noble friend, intoned
The fearsome words. When we were children
We heard them from our nurse. I know them well.

Intoning

Beware of the gods in
Their friendship with us!
The power they hold is
Eternally theirs. They
Are able to use it
According to whim.

For those they exalt
The danger is doubled.
At tables of gold the
Chairs are arranged in
The clouds as on cliff edge.

Should quarrels arise,
The guests are abused and
Disgraced. When they fall to
The depths of the darkest
Abyss they then languish;
They wait there in vain for
Their cause to be heard.

The gods keep on feasting,
Eternal, secure at
Their tables of gold.
They live their exalted
Lives on the peaks,
And out of the chasms,
Arising as steam,
The breath of the Titans,
And choked cries as of victims,
Ascend to their ears.

The rulers avert then
Their gaze, with its blessing,

From all of our line,
Refusing to see in
The grandchildren's features
The silent reminders
Of those they once loved.

This song of the fates
Is heard by the exile
Grown old in dark caverns.
He thinks of his line of
Descendants and sighs
With a shake of his head.

ACT FIVE

Scene One

Arkas and Thoas.

Arkas: I must confess I feel confused, not knowing
Who most deserves my deep suspicion.
The prisoners? Perhaps they're plotting to escape.
The priestess? She's aiding and abetting them?
The rumour's growing that the ship that brought
Them here is hidden somewhere in a bay.
That man's insane behaviour, this consecration,
The holy ritual causing this delay –
They're arousing my suspicion. They put
Me on my guard.

Thoas: Have the priestess come at once. Then along
The shore conduct a thorough, speedy search
Extending from the headland to the temple.
Be careful not to violate the sanctuary.
Then lie in ambush ready to attack.
When they appear, seize them and bring them here. *Exit Arkas.*

Scene Two

Thoas alone.

Thoas: For me her presence was so sacred; and now
The rage within me shifts horribly
From her back to myself. I was too kind
To her, far too indulgent. Now this betrayal.

Slavery a person can accept.
Abolish every trace of freedom and soon
Obedience is learnt. Had she my fathers
To contend with, had she survived their awesome
Rage, too glad to save herself alone
She would have praised her luck, without delay
Have shed the blood of strangers at the altar
And of necessity had made a virtue.
But no, I treated her too kindly and am
Rewarded with presumption. I hoped in vain
To win her for myself. She ponders now
A life of independence. She charmed her way
Into my heart and now, when I oppose
Her she tries to get her way with cunning
And deceit. My kindness? To her it's nothing
New. She takes it all for granted.

Scene Three

Enter Iphigenie.

Iphigenie: You want me? What's the reason for your visit?

Thoas: You have delayed the sacrifice. *Your* reason?

Iphigenie: I have explained it all just now to Arkas.

Thoas: And now you can explain it all to me.

Iphigenie: The goddess leaves you time for due reflection.

Thoas: It seems to me you need some time yourself.

Iphigenie: If you are now unbending in your cruel

Intent, why come to me? To carry out
Inhuman tasks is easy for a King.
Greedy for rewards, some men will share
The curse accompanying their deed. The King
Meantime remains aloof. He's innocent
Of crime. From threatening clouds above, designs
Of death he forms. Through messengers he sends
Down thunderbolts to wreak destruction on
His victim's head. And he, remote above
The storm, floats like a god in his security.

Thoas: A wild song, coming from a priestess!

Iphigenie: Priestess? Remember, the one you chose to honour
Was Agamemnon's unknown daughter. And now
You issue to a princess curt commands?
No! I learnt obedience from childhood –
To parents first, and then to the divinity.
Conforming, I could feel that I was free.
To hard, rough words spoken by
A man I've never had to yield –
In Greece *or* here.

Thoas: The ancient law is what commands, not me.

Iphigenie: We seize on laws which justify our passion.
I hear a different, older law that tells
Me to oppose you: the sacred law
Of hospitality.

Thoas: The prisoners and you are clearly very
Close. Emotion, sympathy make you
Forget a fundamental truth: the weak
Provoke the mighty at their peril.

Iphigenie: Whether I speak or hold my peace, you know
The secrets of my heart. To recognize
A fate just like one's own would open up
The narrowest of hearts. How much more mine!
I see in them myself. I too have trembled,
Kneeling at the altar, prematurely
Facing death, the dagger poised to pierce
My living breast. My life, in terror, whirled
Within me. I fainted – and was saved.
What gods in goodness grant to us, should we
Not feel obliged, where wretchedness prevails,
To grant another? You *know* it. *Me* you know.
So why resort to force?

Thoas: Your duty, not your King, should hold sway.

Iphigenie: My duty! Admit: with naked force you triumph
Over women. By birth I'm free as any
Man. If Agamemnon's son stood facing
You and you insisted where you have
No right, he has a sword, he has the strength
To fight, defend his cause. I have but words.

Thoas: Much more respect I give them than a brother's sword.

Iphigenie: With weapons fortune changes back and forth.
No prudent man will underestimate
His foe, and nature doesn't leave the weak
Defenceless in face of raw aggression.
In nature's cunning they rejoice.
They learn her arts: elude, delay, avoid.
The violent man deserves that these be used.

Thoas: Caution is a counter to your cunning.

Iphigenie: It would not be needed by an upright man.

Thoas: Be careful! Don't bring judgement on yourself!

Iphigenie: Within me, if only you could see the struggle
To avert the evil fate that threatens me.
Do I stand confronting you with no
Defence? Do you reject my plea, the olive
Branch which should be mightier in my hand
Than sword or spear? What means is left?
What can protect my inner self? The goddess
May oblige me with a miracle! – Within
Myself has all resource dried up?

Thoas: The fate of these two strangers, it seems to me,
Has roused in you undue concern. Who are these men,
Tell me, to cause you such excitement?

Iphigenie: They are…they seem…I take them to be Greeks.

Thoas: Your fellow countrymen! And they, no doubt,
Have re-enkindled your desire to return.

Iphigenie: *silent for a moment.*
Momentous deeds – have men alone
The right to them? Does the impossible arise
Nowhere but in the mighty warrior's breast?
What makes an action great? What oft repeated tale
Exalts us, sends shivers down our spines, if not
The story of amazing exploits by
Courageous men? A man who slips alone
At night through enemy lines and, unexpected,
Like a raging flame attacks them sleeping
Or awake, then, cornered, escapes with
Their own horses and with plunder – he

Alone is worthy of our praise? Or he
Who spurns the safest routes and boldly scours
The mountains and the forests to rid the region
Of its robbers? What's left to us? Must women
Abdicate their innate rights and act
Like savages at war with savages
To take from you your dominance with arms,
Avenging our suppression by spilling blood? –
A different kind of daring arises in my
Breast. If I should fail, severe reproach,
And worse, will fall on me:
You gods, to you alone can I entrust
My fate. The truth, they say, is found with you.
If that be so, then show it now. Today,
Here, glorify your truth through me.
And now the King must hear the truth: there is
A secret plot. You ask in vain about
The prisoners. They've gone – to join their friends.
Their ship is by the shore. The older one,
When here a prey to fits, has now been cured.
He is Orestes, my brother; his
Companion is a childhood friend called
Pylades. Apollo sent them to these
Shores from Delphi with divine decree:
To steal the image of Diana, and bring
It back to him. For doing this, Orestes,
Guilty of his mother's blood and hounded
By the furies, will find liberation. Both of us,
Survivors of the house of Tantalus,
I have now placed in your hands. Can you destroy us?

Thoas: You think this rough barbarian, this foreigner,
Will listen to the voice of truth, humanity,
Which Atreus, a Greek, your civilized
Ancestor could not hear?

Iphigenie: This voice is heard by everyone no matter
Where he lives – wherever life flows pure,
Untrammelled, through the human breast.
Thoas, what thoughts are forming deep within you?
Destruction? Then begin with me.   I see
All hope of rescue now has vanished.
My loved ones I have rashly, yet with open
Eyes, delivered to a gruesome fate.
How can I look on them in bonds,
How look into my brother's eyes and bid
Farewell when I have caused his death?
I can never face his gaze again.

Thoas: You've been deceived! They've spun this yarn to take
You in. They know you lack experience,
You're gullible.

Iphigenie: No, Thoas, no! They could have tried
Deceit but they are open, they are honest.
If you find I'm wrong, then execute them
And banish me, for my stupidity,
To some dreary, rocky island. But, if you
Find this man to be my longed for brother,
Release us, extend your magnanimity
Not just to me but to my kin. My father
Fell a victim to his wife and she
A victim to her son. On him depends
The hope of all our line. Let me,
Remaining pure in heart and hand, return
To heal our house. You'll keep your word!
You swore, should once the chance present itself,
You'd let me sail for Greece: and here it is!
A King does not, like other men, to save
Embarrassment, comply with a request

Just to dismiss petitioners, or promise
On conditions he hopes will never be fulfilled.
His dignity is at its height when he
Bestows the long-awaited gift.

Thoas: As fire and water, hissing, clash with one
Another, so anger in my heart confronts
Your words.

Iphigenie: May your mercy and magnanimity
Shine like a sacred lamp on me, amid
Songs of praise and joy and gratitude.

Thoas: This voice – how often it has calmed me down!

Iphigenie: As a sign of peace give me your hand.

Thoas: You ask a lot within so short a time.

Iphigenie: A generous deed is done without reflection.

Thoas: Not so! Such deeds can have their ill effects.

Iphigenie: Yes, where doubt can shed its baleful light.
Don't hesitate! Do what your instinct says!

Scene Four

Enter Orestes, armed.

Orestes: *speaking towards the wings.*
Redouble your efforts. Hold back the enemy
A minute more. I need protection for
My sister till she's on the ship. (*To Iphigenie*) Be quick!

Our time is running out! *He notices the King.*

Thoas: *reaching for his sword.*
In *my* presence *no* man bears a naked
Sword unpunished.

Iphigenie: Don't defile Diana's temple
With murderous rage. Command your people
To put down their arms. Listen to your priestess,
To your sister.

Orestes: Tell me, who is this who threatens us?

Iphigenie: Respect in him the king, my second father.
Orestes, forgive me what I've done. With childlike
Trust I've put our fate entirely in
His hands. In telling him your plans
I've freed myself of guilt, of treachery.

Orestes: Is he prepared to let us go in peace?

Iphigenie: Put up your naked sword if I'm to answer.

Orestes: *sheathing his sword.*
Then speak. As you can see, I'm listening.

Scene Five

Enter Pylades. Soon after him, Arkas. Both with swords drawn.

Pylades: Come on, hurry up. Our men are making
A last-ditch stand. The enemy are forcing
A gradual retreat. The sea – (*breaks off*)
What have we here? A council of rulers?

The venerable King himself is present!

Arkas: My King, before your enemies you stand
There calmly, as is fitting. The rashness
Of their deeds will soon be punished. Their men
Are routed. We have their ship. One word from you
And up it goes in flames.

Thoas: Go! Restrain our people. Avoid
Hostilities until we've talked. *Exit Arkas.*

Orestes: All right! – Pylades, my friend, gather
The surviving men together. Stand back calmly
And see what fate the gods decree for us. *Exit Pylades.*

Scene Six

Iphigenie. Thoas. Orestes.

Iphigenie: Before you start to talk I need
Your reassurance. I fear a fierce quarrel
Will ensue unless you, my King, will hear
The voice of mildness, and you, my brother,
Will restrain your youthful impulse.

Thoas: My anger, as befits the older man,
I can restrain. Now, answer me. What proof
Is there that you are Agamemnon's son
And brother to this priestess.

Orestes: Here is the sword with which he
Vanquished Troy's brave men. It is the sword
I wrested from his murderer. I prayed
To have the courage, strength, and fortune of this

Great King, and sought for myself a better death
Than his. Select the best, the noblest
Of your warriors to pit against me.
Wherever the earth nourishes heroic sons
This wish is not refused to strangers.

Thoas: Our ancient law has never granted
This privilege to strangers.

Orestes: Then let us make a new decree!
The noble deed performed before them by
Their rulers will be enshrined by subjects as
Their law. This fight for freedom should not
Be just for us. Let me, the stranger, fight
For every stranger. Should I lose, then let their
Condemnation coincide with mine.
But, should I win, let every stranger to
These shores be greeted with love
And hospitality and then allowed
To go his way.

Thoas: You seem to me, young man, quite worthy of
Your ancestors – the ones you claim to spring from.
You see around us brave and noble men,
But I myself can still confront a foe.
Against your skills and strength I'll pit my own.

Iphigenie: Thoas, Thoas! The problem can be solved
Without recourse to blood. Reflect a moment
On my plight. One thrust brings death, a hero's
Death in glory. But no one glorifies
The streams of tears the grieving woman sheds.
The poet passes over the thousand days
And nights she weeps. In vain she would call back
The deadly stroke inflicted on her friend.

I, too, was worried that perhaps a treacherous
Ruse would tear me from the safety of
The temple and leave me languish as a slave.
I quizzed them, in great detail, asked for signs,
And now I am convinced. His right hand
Bears a mark – three stars.
That destined him to grievous deeds – the priest
Said at his birth. A further sign: this scar
That splits his eyebrow. When he was young
Electra let him fall from her unsteady
Grasp. He struck his head against a tripod.
This *is* Orestes. As further witness should
I name the strong resemblance with his father,
The way my heart exults within me when
I see him?

Thoas: But even should your words remove all doubt,
And should the urge within me be contained,
We still must let the sword decide. I see
No peace. You said yourself they've come to steal
From me the statue of Diana. You don't
Expect that I will let this happen? Your cultured
People often look with lustful eyes
On treasures we barbarians hold dear:
The golden fleece, our horses, our daughters…
And yet, not always did their violence
And cunning see them safely home.

Orestes: The statue, King, is not what should divide us.
I understand the error in which, as in
A veil, the god Apollo had wrapped our minds
When he instructed us to travel here.
"The sister, brought back to Greece from where,
Amongst the Taurians, she stays against
Her will, has power to remove your family's

Curse." We thought he meant the statue of
His sister. But *(turning to Iphigenie)* you're the one he meant.
The curse could not sustain its iron grip.
You are restored to your beloved kin.
You touched me – I was healed.
In your embrace I felt the evil claws
Within take hold and shatter me one last time,
And then my persecutor fled like a serpent
To its hole. And now the brilliant light
Of day through you I can enjoy. Diana's
Plan was beautiful, was glorious.
Like a sacred image to which by god's
Decree the destiny of a town is tied
She spirited you away to be protectress
Of our line, preserved you as priestess in
Seclusion, a blessing for your brother
And your kin. And now, when rescue seems
Completely out of reach, all is restored
To us through you. – King Thoas, look on us
With eyes of peace. Allow her to fulfil
Her role, to purify our house, atone
For me, then place my father's crown
Upon my head. She brought you blessing. Now
Return it. Give your blessing to us both.
The boast of men is force and cunning,
But these are overshadowed by the truth,
The clear integrity, the childlike trust
The priestess manifests to such a noble man.

Iphigenie: Remember your promise. These words,
Just spoken by a man so straight and true,
You hear. Now look at us. How rarely
You are called upon for such a noble deed.
Don't miss the chance: the moment is at hand.

Thoas: Then go!

Iphigenie: Not so, my Thoas. Without your blessing, against
Your will I'll not depart from you –
Not as an exile. Between us we should
Uphold the law of friendship.
And so our parting is not final.
I've looked up to you as to my father,
And this will never change.
At home, if I should hear the sound
Of Taurian speech or see men dressed the way
Your people dress, no matter who they are
I'll look on them as gods. A place to rest
I'll make for them myself. I'll seat them
By the fire and, avid in my questions,
Will ask them: "What of Thoas? Has he prospered?"
Oh, may the gods be rich with their rewards
For deeds so generous, so mild as yours.
Goodbye! Don't turn away. Speak a fond
Farewell. And then the sails will gently billow
And tears will flow to ease the pain of parting.
Goodbye. (*Offering her hand*) *Your* hand, in token of our
friendship.

Thoas: Farewell!